HOW DID WE FIND OUT ABOUT
VITAMINS?

HOW DID WE FIND OUT . . . SERIES
Each of the books in this series on the
history of science emphasizes the process of
discovery.

"How Did We Find Out" Books by
Isaac Asimov

HOW DID WE FIND OUT
THE EARTH IS ROUND?

HOW DID WE FIND OUT ABOUT
ELECTRICITY?

HOW DID WE FIND OUT ABOUT
NUMBERS?

HOW DID WE FIND OUT ABOUT
DINOSAURS?

HOW DID WE FIND OUT ABOUT
GERMS?

HOW DID WE FIND OUT ABOUT
VITAMINS?

HOW DID WE FIND OUT

ABOUT VITAMINS?

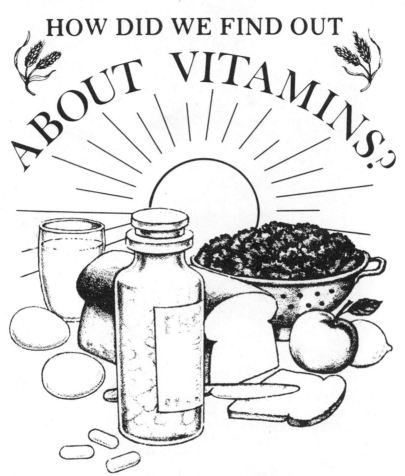

Isaac Asimov
Illustrated by David Wool

WALKER AND COMPANY
New York

To the talented Bruce Bennetts

First published in the United States of America in 1974 by the Walker Publishing Company, Inc.

Published simultaneously in Canada by Fitzhenry & Whiteside, Limited, Toronto.

Trade ISBN: 0-8027-6183-6
Reinf. ISBN: 0-8027-6184-4

LIBRARY OF CONGRESS CATALOG CARD NUMBER: 73-92453

PRINTED IN THE UNITED STATES OF AMERICA

CONTENTS

1 Disease and Diet

AFTER CHRISTOPHER COLUMBUS discovered America in 1492, European nations began to send out ships on long voyages across the oceans. The little sailing ships of those days often stayed away from land for many weeks at a time.

While they were at sea, sailors ate the food that was stored on shipboard. Those were the days before refrigeration, so the ship could carry only food that would not spoil at ordinary temperatures. They ate dry bread and dried or smoked meats. Although the diet was very dull, there was usually enough food, and the sailors didn't go hungry.

However, sailors often became sick on those long voyages. They got weak, their gums started to bleed, their muscles hurt. After a while they got too weak to work and finally many died. The disease was called "scurvy," but no one knows where the name comes from.

Scurvy also struck in prisons and hospitals where the same kind of cheap food was eaten day after day.

It was found in armies and in besieged cities—
wherever the diet was dull and monotonous. Every
once in a while, someone would notice this connection between scurvy and diet.

In 1734, for instance, an Austrian doctor, J.G.H.
Kramer, was serving with the army when an epidem-
ic of scurvy broke out. He noticed that it was always

**SAILOR
WITH SCURVY**

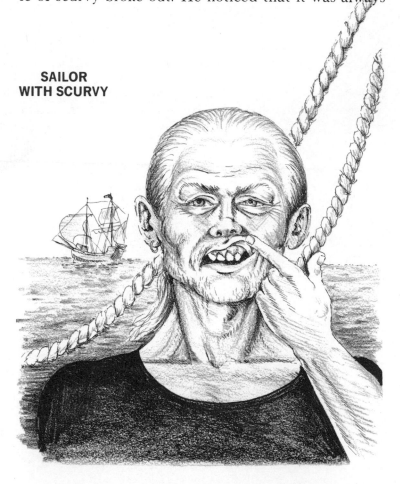

the common soldiers who got it, never the officers. The common soldiers had only bread and beans to eat, but the officers also ate fruits and green vegetables.

In 1737, Kramer wrote a report saying that fruits and vegetables would prevent scurvy. Hardly anyone paid attention, however, and scurvy continued to strike.

The British government was particularly worried about scurvy. In the 1700s, the British were establishing colonies all over the world. They led other nations in trading on the high seas. They needed many merchant ships to carry goods and many warships to protect their trade and their colonies. Yet on all these ships sailors were frequently attacked by scurvy, which left the ships with poorly-working crews.

A Scottish doctor, James Lind, became interested in this problem. He came across Kramer's report, and then he went through old books to find out more about scurvy. For instance, back in 1537, a French explorer, Jacques Cartier (kahr-TYAY), had landed in Canada with a crew that were almost all dead from scurvy. The Indians gave them water in which evergreen needles had been soaked. To everyone's amazement they recovered.

Lind decided that scurvy could be stopped by the right diet. In 1747, he began to experiment with sailors who had scurvy to see what kind of diet would best cure them. In some cases, he added cider to the regular diet, in others vinegar, in still others various fruit juices. He found that the quickest recovery came when juice from citrus fruits—oranges, lemons, or limes—was added to the diet.

He announced this and began campaigning to get the British navy to add these fruit juices to the diet of its sailors. He could not get the navy to agree, however. The notion seemed too new and strange.

A great British explorer, Captain James Cook, *was* impressed. He included limes with the food stores on board his ships and made his men drink the juice when they were ill. In the great Pacific voyages he made in the 1770s, he lost only one man from scurvy. *Still*, the British navy didn't change its ways.

Dr. Lind died in 1794 and the year after his death the British navy gave way. Great Britain was fighting a war with France and was anxious about losing British sailors weakened by scurvy. Limes were taken aboard the warships.

From 1795 on, scurvy was wiped out in the British navy. The use of limes on British warships became so common that British sailors were called "limeys." A section of the London docks where limes were stored was called "Limehouse."

A hundred years later, the Japanese navy faced a similar problem.

Japan had first learned about western ways in 1853, when American ships sailed into Tokyo harbor and demanded that the nation trade with the rest of the world. Japan agreed, and quickly reorganized herself in western fashion. She built western-style warships of her own and developed a navy.

Japanese sailors often fell sick with a disease called

**CARTIER'S CREW
BEING TREATED
BY INDIANS**

11

**WHITE RICE WAS A STAPLE
OF THE JAPANESE DIET**

"beriberi," (BEH-ree-BEH-ree). This is a word from the language used on the island of Ceylon and it means "great weakness." People with beriberi become very weak and their arms and legs are almost paralyzed. Finally, they die.

Beriberi is not the same as scurvy, however. The weakness shows in a different way, affecting the lower legs particularly. Beriberi can occur even when some vegetables and fruit juices are part of the sailor's diet.

In 1878, beriberi became so common on Japanese warships that one-third of the men were out of action. Japan would have been unable to fight a war.

The admiral in charge of the Japanese navy, K. Takake (TAK-kah-kee), knew that the British had beaten the scurvy problem by changing the diet of their sailors. He also knew that British sailors never got beriberi. He therefore compared the diet of British and Japanese sailors.

Japanese sailors ate some vegetables, fish, and white rice. The British sailors did not eat rice, but ate other grains such as barley. Takake made the Japanese sailors eat barley along with their rice. The result was the disappearance of beriberi from the Japanese navy.

Neither Dr. Lind nor Admiral Takake knew *why* a change in diet prevented a disease from striking or cured it once it had struck. Neither did anyone else at the time.

During the 1800s, though, chemists began to study food to see what it was made of. They discovered five main substances in food: 1) carbohydrates, such as sugar and starch; 2) lipids, such as fats and oils; 3) proteins; 4) minerals; 5) water. That seemed to include everything, and each kind of substance was useful to the body.

Suppose, then, you started with some carbohydrate, lipid, protein, and minerals and mixed them all with water in the proper proportions. You would make a kind of artificial food. Would such an artificial food keep people alive?

There was a chance to find out in 1870. A German army had surrounded Paris and the Parisian people were starving. A French chemist, Jean Dumas (doo-MAH), was in the city at the time. He tried to prepare such an artificial food, hoping it would substitute for the milk that babies needed but could not get. It didn't work.

In 1871, Dumas wrote about his experiment and suggested that there might be something in food besides carbohydrates, lipids, proteins, minerals, and water; something else that was essential for life and health. Naturally, it would have to be present in very small quantities, or chemists would have found it.

In 1880, a German chemist, N. Lunin (LOO-nin), also prepared an artificial food. He fed a mixture of protein, sugar, minerals, and water to mice. They didn't live long.

He tried a different artificial food. He separated the protein, sugar, fat, and minerals from milk. He then put them together again and added the right amount of water. It seemed he had artificial milk, but when he fed it to mice, they still didn't live long. Yet when he fed the mice on milk exactly as it came from the cow, the mice lived on and on. Lunin concluded that there were substances in the milk *besides* carbohydrates, lipids, proteins, minerals, and water and that these substances were necessary to life and health.

If scientists had listened to Dumas and to Lunin, they might have found an explanation for scurvy and beriberi. Perhaps lime juice contained a small quantity of a substance necessary to life and health, and without it people suffered from scurvy. Perhaps barley contained a small quantity of another substance necessary to life and health, and without it people suffered from beriberi.

One of the reasons doctors didn't listen to Dumas and Lunin was that they were going off in another direction. In the late 1800s, doctors had discovered that many diseases were caused by germs.° For a while, they couldn't help thinking that *all* disease was caused by germs.

For instance, they thought that scurvy and beriberi were caused by germs. They knew that a change in diet prevented or cured these two diseases, but they couldn't believe this to be important. Perhaps the change in diet just helped the body fight off the germs.

So for a while, doctors looked for scurvy and beriberi germs. They did very little to discover more about the substances in food, whose absence can cause disease, as we now know.

°See *How Did We Find Out About Germs?* (Walker, 1974).

2 The First Vitamin

IN THE 1890s, the search for the beriberi germ reached the large islands off southeast Asia that make up the modern nation of Indonesia. In those days, the islands were controlled by the Netherlands and were called the Dutch East Indies. The chief island of the group is Java.

As was true in many lands in eastern and southern Asia, the people of those islands frequently suffered from beriberi. A Dutch doctor, Christian Eijkman (IKE-man), went to Java to search for the germ that might be causing beriberi.

The doctor failed. He could find no germ that was present in people with beriberi and not present in people without the disease.

Then, in 1896, some of the chickens which were kept at the hospital grew ill. They suffered from a nerve disease called "polyneuritis" (POL-ee-nyoo-RY-tis). As a result of this disease, they showed the kind of weakness that was caused by beriberi. In fact, beriberi is a kind of human polyneuritis.

Eijkman was pleased with this new development. He felt that if he could find the germ that was causing polyneuritis in the chickens, it would be the same germ that caused beriberi in human beings.

He began to search for germs in the sick chickens. He injected those that he found into healthy chickens to see whether he could give them polyneuritis. He failed, but he kept on trying.

Then, suddenly, all the chickens got better. There were no more sick chickens for Eijkman to work with. What had happened?

Eijkman investigated. He found that just before the chickens got sick, the person in charge of them had begun to give them food left over by the patients in the hospital. This included white rice.

When rice grows, the grains are covered with a brownish husk. With the husk left on, it is called "brown rice." This husk contains oils which can get rancid, so if brown rice is stored it quickly spoils. If the husk is polished off, the white grain underneath

CHICKEN WITH POLYNEURITIS

NORMAL CHICKEN

("white rice") is exposed. It can keep for a long time without going bad, so people in rice-eating countries usually polish the rice in order to store it. Asian people are used to eating white rice and don't like brown rice.

It was this white rice that had been given to the chickens. After they ate white rice for a while they got polyneuritis.

Then the man in charge of the food supply for the hospital was transferred. The new man who replaced him did not feel that good food used for human beings should be wasted on chickens. He began to feed the chickens on cheap brown rice that the patients wouldn't eat—and, surprisingly enough, they got well.

Eijkman considered this and decided to try an experiment. He began with a few healthy chickens and fed them on white rice. After a while, they became sick with polyneuritis. He then fed them on brown rice. They quickly got better. Eijkman did this over and over. He could make chickens sick any time he wanted. He could make them well again any time he wanted.

Lind and Takake had each shown that an illness could be *cured* by a particular diet. Eijkman was the first person who managed to *produce* an illness by a particular diet.

What did it mean, though? At the time, all the illnesses that doctors knew about were caused by *something*. People became ill because a poison had gotten into the body, or a germ. Eijkman had not found a germ for beriberi, so he thought it must be caused by a poison. He decided that grains of white rice had some poison in them that made people or chickens ill, and that the rice husks had something that neutralized the poison and made people and chickens well again.

Another Dutch doctor, Gerrit Grijns (GRINEZ), who had been working with Eijkman, disagreed. He felt it was the other way around. In 1901, he suggested that the trouble was that something the body needed was *not* present in rice grains and *was* present in the rice husk. If anyone ate too much white rice and not enough rice husks, he or she would get sick because the white rice lacked certain substances.

The body is like a machine that needs a few drops of oil now and then to keep its moving parts sliding against each other smoothly. If those few drops aren't added, the machine starts grinding and squealing. That is not because something damaging has been added to it, but because something necessary has been left out.

For the first time, then, it began to seem possible that a living organism could grow ill from the *lack* of something—a deficiency of an important ingredient. Beriberi might be considered a "deficiency disease" for that reason.

In 1906, an English chemist, Frederick Gowland Hopkins, studied deficiency diseases. In a lecture he gave at a scientific meeting, he suggested that there might be many substances in food that were present in very small quantities. The human body could not make these substances for itself but had to have the small quantities ready made in its food. If those small quantities were missing, illness would result.

BERIBERI VICTIM

SIR FREDERICK GOWLAND HOPKINS

A lack of each different substance would give rise to a different deficiency disease. Hopkins suggested that beriberi was one of these diseases, and that scurvy was another. He suggested a third disease, called "rickets." This is a disease in which children's bones grow soft so that they twist and become misshapen. (The word "rickets" is from an old English word meaning "twisted.")

Hopkins was a very important chemist. When he said he believed in the notion of deficiency diseases, many other scientists took the idea seriously and began to look for evidence to back him up.

Suppose Grijns and Hopkins were right and there was a substance in rice husks that the body needed to prevent beriberi—an "anti-beriberi substance"? If so, what could it be? Could it be separated from the rest of the material in the husk?

One thing chemists could try was to soak the husk in water. Some of the substances in the husk would pass into the water and "dissolve." If the anti-beriberi substance dissolved in the water, then the water could perhaps cure beriberi in human beings or polyneuritis in birds. Eijkman and Grijns tried this in 1906 and found the water cured pigeons with polyneuritis.

In that way, they showed the anti-beriberi substance to be "water-soluble." They had also separated it from those parts of the husk that were *not* water-soluble and did not soak into the water.

What next? Suppose certain chemicals were added to the water that had the various water-soluble substances of rice husks, including the anti-beriberi substance? These chemicals might combine with some of the substances but not others. The new chemical combination might settle at the bottom of the water as a sediment. Then you could work with sick pigeons and test whether the cure for polyneuritis was still in the water (in solution), or whether it was in the sediment. If it was still in the water, you could add another chemical and see whether that would combine with the anti-beriberi substance. If it was already in the sediment, you could work with that.

By trying various chemicals in the water in which rice husks have been soaked and by continually checking to see which part of the sediment, or the solution, cures pigeon polyneuritis, you would eventually find the pure anti-beriberi substance.

In 1912, a group of Japanese chemists, headed by Umetaro Suzuki (soo-ZOO-kee), managed to combine a small amount of anti-beriberi substance with a certain chemical. A tiny dose of about 1/3000 of an ounce cured polyneuritis in a pigeon.

Now there was another question. What was the chemical structure of the anti-beriberi substance? Every substance is made up of identical small objects called "molecules." Molecules are so tiny that they cannot be seen in ordinary microscopes. Even so, molecules are made up of still smaller objects called "atoms." Each molecule is made up of different numbers of different atoms which are connected in a particular way.

The kind of molecules in living beings can be very complicated. Each molecule can contain dozens or even hundreds of atoms, all connected in a unique

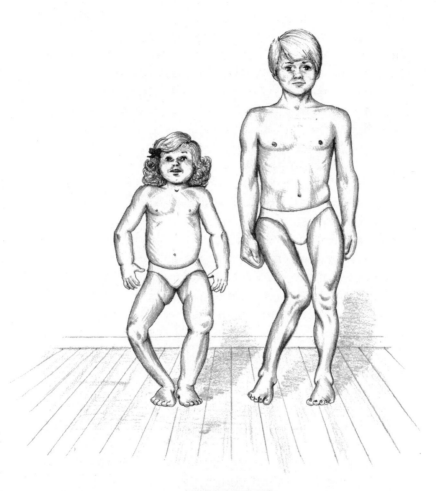

**DEFORMITIES
CAUSED BY RICKETS**

way. Chemists had to find out three things: how many atoms there were in each molecule of the anti-beriberi substance; what different kinds of atoms and how many of each were present; and finally, how they were all hooked together. If they could discover that, they would know the chemical structure.

There was so little of the anti-beriberi substance to experiment with, and the molecule was so complicated, that it took about a quarter of a century to work out the chemical structure.

Still, a beginning was made in 1912. A Polish chemist, Casimir Funk, who was working in England, showed that the anti-beriberi substance reacted with other chemicals as though it had a well-known three-atom combination as part of its molecule. This three-atom combination was known to chemists as an "amine group." Any substance that contained this group was called an "amine" (ah-MEEN). Funk said that the anti-beriberi substance was an amine that was essential for life. He guessed that the other substances needed in small quantities, to cure such illnesses as scurvy and rickets, were also amines.

He suggested a fourth disease that might also be the result of a deficiency of some substance in the diet. This disease was "pellagra" (from Italian words meaning "rough skin"). It was common in Italy and in the southern parts of the United States; people suffering from it had rough, red skin, an inflamed tongue, and a kind of beriberi.

Funk thought the anti-pellagra substance might be an amine, too. There were a whole series of amines, he thought, that were needed in small quantities for

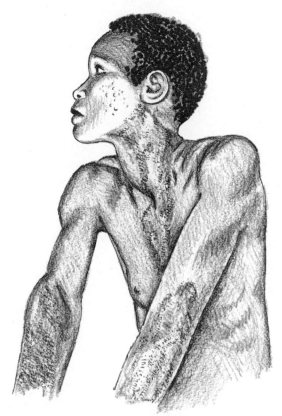

PELLAGRA VICTIM

life and health. Since the Latin word for life is "vita," Funk called them all "vitamines."

It was eventually found, however, that some of these substances were not amines. For that reason, the name was changed in 1920. The "e" was dropped so that there would be less similarity to "amine." The name, invented by Funk, became "vitamin" and we have used that name ever since. The very first vitamin that chemists and doctors studied in detail was the anti-beriberi substance.

3 Many More Vitamins

AFTER EIJKMAN'S DISCOVERY of the anti-beriberi substance, more and more chemists began to study diets
in order to identify those substances needed for life
in small quantities.

One way to do this was to feed white rats on care-
fully-prepared diets. Rats were used because they
were easy to keep in cages, they were small and did
not require much food, and they had many young so
that there was always a big supply of them. Then,
too, they ate the same sort of food that human beings
ate. If rats needed some particular substance to stay
alive, it was a good guess that human beings also
did.

Two American chemists, Elmer Verner McCollum
and Marguerite Davis, were working with rats in
1913. They found that on certain diets in which mix-
tures of sugar, proteins, and minerals were used the
rats stopped growing. If, however, a little bit of butter or egg-yolk were added to the diet, they grew and
acted healthy.

Something was present in butter or egg-yolk that
seemed to be necessary for normal growth. Whatever

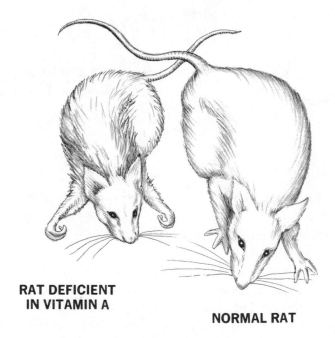

**RAT DEFICIENT
IN VITAMIN A**

NORMAL RAT

it was, however, did not soak out of the butter or egg-yolk into water. The substance was *not* water-soluble.

The substances in food fall into two classes. Some substances dissolve in water but do not dissolve in fat. These are water-soluble substances. Other substances dissolve in fat but do not dissolve in water. These are fat-soluble substances.

Since the material needed to keep rats growing was in fatty material like butter and egg-yolk, it was not surprising that it would not dissolve in water. However, substances that are fat-soluble and will not dissolve in water can often be dissolved in a chemical called "ether."

When butter or egg-yolk was soaked in ether, the substance needed for growth passed into the ether. McCollum and Davis knew that rats grew and were healthy when this substance was added to the rats' diet.

At first, McCollum and Davis did not notice any special illness in rats that lacked the fat-soluble substance in their diet. The rats just stopped growing.

Later that same year, however, two other American chemists, Thomas Burr Osborne and Lafayette Benedict Mendel, continued to experiment and found that rats which lacked this fat-soluble substance in their diet had trouble with their eyes. Their eyes grew dry and inflamed.

A similar disease was known to occur sometimes in human beings. Not only did the eyes become inflamed, but people who were ill in this way had trouble seeing in dim light, especially at night, so the disease was called "night-blindness."

It seemed then that there were two different vitamins. There was a fat-soluble vitamin which cured night-blindness, and there was a water-soluble vitamin which cured beriberi.

Two different vitamins deserved two different names. In order to find a sensible name for a chemical, chemists like to know just how the atoms in a molecule are arranged. From the arrangement, they think up some name that fits.

There was no chance of that, however, in 1913. No one knew what the atom arrangement in the vitamin molecules were. They knew that they might not find out for a long time. McCollum and Davis decided to

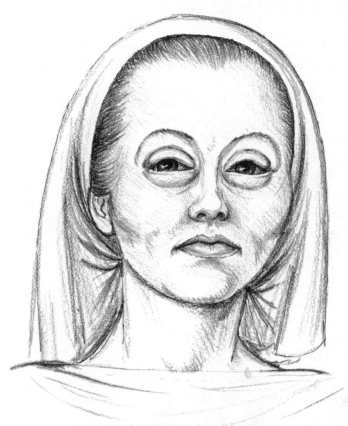

**EYE DISEASE CAUSED BY
LACK OF VITAMIN A**

avoid giving the vitamins real names. They would just use letters of the alphabet.

They called the fat-soluble vitamin which they had discovered "Vitamin A." They called the water-soluble anti-beriberi substance "Vitamin B." It was in this way that letters began to be used for the names of vitamins.

Scientists were also wondering whether there was a vitamin that cured scurvy. After Eijkman's discovery of the anti-beriberi substance, the search for an anti-scurvy substance began.

One way to check on an anti-scurvy substance would be to separate the different parts of orange juice and try it out on people who were sick with scurvy.

However, hardly anyone had scurvy anymore and you could not very well ask someone to get it by living on a deficient diet. In the first place, scurvy is a serious and painful disease and people might not want to volunteer. Secondly, it would take too long, since scurvy develops only slowly.

The thing to do was to experiment on animals. Animals can more easily be kept on special diets than human beings can. The trouble was that animals did not seem to get scurvy. A diet that would give a human being scurvy would not give a rat or a chicken scurvy. Either rats and chickens had no need for the anti-scurvy vitamin at all, or else they made it for themselves in their own bodies.

Fortunately, a German doctor, Axel Holst, and an Austrian chemist, Alfred Frohlich (FRO-lik) who were working on the problem, discovered by 1912 that guinea pigs could get scurvy. They are the only animals except for men, apes, and monkeys that can. In fact, guinea pigs get scurvy even more easily than men do. Holst and Frohlich found that guinea pigs got scurvy if they ate nothing but grain. If, however, some cabbage was added to their diet, they did not get the disease.

Now it was possible to track down the anti-scurvy substance. It turned out to be water-soluble, as Vitamin B was, but it was not at all like Vitamin B. For one thing, Vitamin B was a sturdy substance. Its molecule did not change easily. If it was dissolved in water and then boiled, it could still do its anti-beriberi work after the solution had cooled down.

The anti-scurvy substance was different. If it was dissolved in water and then boiled for half an hour, its molecule underwent changes. It could no longer cure scurvy. That alone showed that the anti-scurvy substance was different from Vitamin B.

In 1920, an English chemist, Jack Cecil Drummond (who was the first to suggest dropping the "e" in "vitamine," since Vitamin A did not have an amine group in its molecules) suggested that the anti-scurvy substance have a letter of its own. He called it "Vitamin C," and it has been called that ever since.

What about rickets? Both Hopkins and Funk thought it might be a vitamin-deficiency disease also. For a long time doctors had known that some substances added to the diet would prevent rickets. Just as lime juice could prevent scurvy, so the oily material from the liver of a codfish ("cod-liver oil") could prevent rickets.

The anti-rickets substance was present in fatty material, so it must be fat-soluble like Vitamin A. Could Vitamin A be the anti-rickets substance? After all, there is Vitamin A in cod-liver oil. A number of foods which prevented night-blindness and, therefore, contained Vitamin A also prevented rickets.

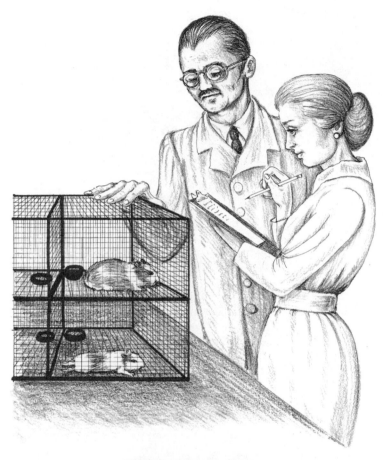

**SCURVY EXPERIMENTS
WITH GUINEA PIGS**

BUBBLING OXYGEN THROUGH COD LIVER OIL

But could one vitamin prevent two such different diseases as night-blindness and rickets? Or were there two vitamins which just happened to be present in the same foods? Was there any way one could test whether there was one vitamin or two?

In 1920, Hopkins found that when the gas, oxygen, was bubbled through melted butter and the butter was then cooled, it no longer prevented night-blindness. Vitamin A was destroyed when it was heated in the presence of oxygen.

Since cod-liver oil also contained Vitamin A, McCollum (who had discovered Vitamin A) decided in 1922 to try passing oxygen through hot cod-liver oil. When it was cooled down, it could no longer prevent night-blindness. The Vitamin A in it was destroyed.

The cod-liver oil which had been heated with oxygen could still prevent rickets, however! The anti-rickets substance had *not* been destroyed and, therefore, it could not be Vitamin A. It had to be a new vitamin, and McCollum called it "Vitamin D."

That left pellagra, which Funk had predicted was a vitamin-deficiency disease.

Pellagra certainly seemed to be cured by diet. In the south of the United States, poor people sometimes could not afford milk for their children. The children developed pellagra. If milk were added to their diet, the pellagra was cured.

An American doctor, Joseph Goldberger, was particularly interested in this. In 1915, he arranged to test a group of eleven men who were in prison in the state of Mississippi. He got them to eat only the food he told them to eat, and he persuaded the Governor to pardon the men if they cooperated.

For half a year, the prisoners ate a diet that lacked milk or meat, and at the end of the time seven of them had definite symptoms of pellagra. They were then fed meat and milk, and after a while they became well again.

This made it look as if the lack of a vitamin might be the cause. To track it down, however, meant an animal had to be found that would develop the disease. In 1916, an American veterinarian, T.N. Spencer, showed that a well-known dog disease, called "blacktongue," was the same as pellagra in human beings.

It soon became certain, from work on blacktongue that the anti-pellagra substance was a water-soluble vitamin. It did not get an ordinary letter name, though. Goldberger called it the "P-P factor" for "pellagra-preventive" and that name was kept for many years.

The use of letter names was becoming clumsy, anyway, as more and more different vitamins were found.

In 1922, two Americans, Herbert McLean Evans and K.J. Scott, discovered a certain fat-soluble vitamin that was neither Vitamin A nor Vitamin D. Without it, rats couldn't give birth to young. Evans and Scott called it "Vitamin E."

Later on, still another fat-soluble vitamin was reported, and it was called "Vitamin F." That turned out to be a false alarm, however, and to this day there is no Vitamin F.

In fact, there have been vitamins reported with letters all the way up to P, but most of them have turned out to be mistakes. The only real vitamin beyond Vitamin E is Vitamin K, which was discovered in 1929 by a Danish chemist, Henrik Dam.

Here is another complication. For a number of

DR. JOSEPH GOLDBERGER

years, some chemists felt that Vitamin B wasn't just a single substance. It prevented beriberi, but there was some evidence that it also contained substances that had no effect on beriberi but that prevented other kinds of illnesses. Perhaps it was a complex vitamin that contained other vitamins?

In 1927, an American named William Davis Salmon prepared a sample of Vitamin B that prevented beriberi but did not help rats grow normally the way ordinary Vitamin B did. He also prepared a sample of Vitamin B that helped rats grow but did not prevent beriberi.

Salmon gave a name to this new vitamin that didn't work on beriberi. He called it "Vitamin G." Other chemists, however, didn't think that was a proper name. They felt that the new vitamin was so like the old Vitamin B that both vitamins ought to have similar names.

The Vitamin B that prevented beriberi was called "Vitamin B_1," therefore, and the new vitamin that kept rats growing, "Vitamin B_2."

As it turned out, the original Vitamin B did not contain just these two vitamins, either, but included a whole group of them. Chemists began to speak of the "B complex" for that reason. Goldberger's "P-P factor" turned out to be a member of the B complex.

Numbering the different vitamins of the B complex proved just as confusing as the lettering. At one time or another, chemists reported the finding of vitamins to which they gave numbers all the way up to B_{14}. Most of these turned out to be mistakes. In fact, except for B_1 and B_2, there are only two other important letter-number combinations.

In 1934, a Hungarian doctor, Paul Gyorgy (DYAWR-gee), found that rats got a skin-disease if they were missing a certain substance. He called that substance "Vitamin B_6." In 1927, two American doctors, George Richards Minot and William Parry Murphy, discovered there was something in liver that could prevent a serious blood disease called "pernicious anemia." The substance that prevented it was eventually named "Vitamin B_{12}."

4 Coenzymes and Vitamins

WHY ARE VITAMINS NECESSARY to life in such small quantities? A thousandth of an ounce, or less, of each vitamin is all we need each day. What can the body do with so little? And if the body can get along with so little, why can't it do without them altogether?

One other type of substance the body needs very little of is the "enzymes." These are substances that help make chemical reactions take place in the body. Each different chemical reaction has its own enzyme. It takes only a tiny quantity of enzyme to make the chemical reaction work.

Are vitamins like enzymes? Apparently not. Enzymes are made up of proteins, which have giant molecules that the body can make for itself. Vitamins have much smaller molecules that the body cannot make for itself.

In 1904, however, a British chemist, Arthur Harden, was working with an enzyme that could bring about changes in a sugar molecule. He placed the enzyme in a bag made of a thin membrane. There were tiny holes in the membrane that small molecules could pass through. The large protein molecules of the enzyme could *not* go through, however.

Harden placed the bag of enzyme in water and the small molecules that were present passed through the membrane into the outside water. The protein molecules of the enzyme stayed put inside the bag, yet

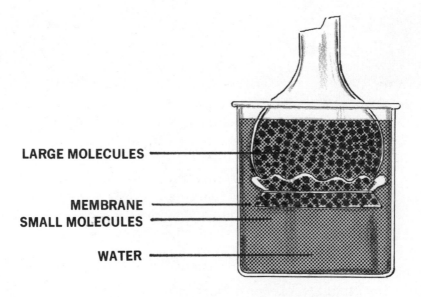

LARGE MOLECULES

MEMBRANE
SMALL MOLECULES

WATER

**Small molecules of the coenzyme
pass through the membrane.**

The larger enzyme molecules stay inside.

they could no longer do the work of an enzyme. Harden took the water from outside the bag and placed it inside the bag. Now the enzyme did its work again.

Harden figured out what had happened. The enzyme is made up of protein molecules, but in order to do its work, it must make use of some small molecule that is not protein. Harden called the small molecule a "coenzyme" because the prefix "co" means "with," and the small molecule worked *with* the enzyme.

If the enzyme is placed in a bag made of thin membrane, the small molecules of the coenzyme leak out into the water. Without the coenzyme, the enzyme cannot do its work. If the water from outside, which contains the coenzyme, is placed into the bag again, the enzyme has its coenzyme and can do its work.

Some enzymes do not have coenzymes. The protein molecule does all the work itself. Many enzymes do have coenzymes, however, and in the years after Harden's discovery, a number of coenzymes were discovered. Since the body needs only small quantities of enzymes, it also needs only small quantities of coenzymes.

Was it possible that the vitamins, which are not proteins and are needed only in small quantities by the body, have something to do with coenzymes, which are also not proteins and are needed only in small quantities by the body? Chemists could not tell until they found out the atomic structure of vitamins and of coenzymes—and that was a hard job.

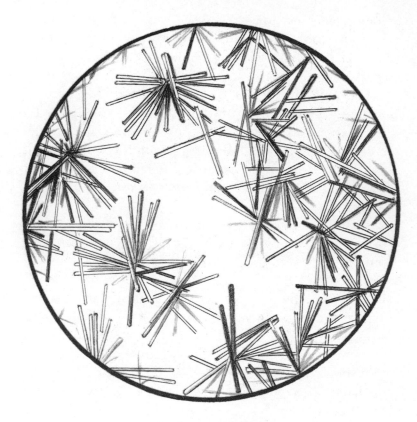

VITAMIN B₁ CRYSTALS

It took forty years after the discovery of the first vitamin by Eijkman to find out its atomic structure. One of the reasons it took so long was that there is so little of the vitamins in food. If chemists started with a whole ton of rice husks, they ended up with about a fifth of an ounce of Vitamin B_1.

Little by little, though, chemists learned about the

$$\begin{array}{c}
\text{N=C—NH}_2 \text{ HCL} \\
\end{array}$$

MOLECULAR STRUCTURE OF THIAMINE

atom arrangements in Vitamin B_1. In 1932, for instance, it was found that among the three dozen atoms in the Vitamin B_1 molecule there was one sulfur atom.

Finally, in 1934, the American chemist, Robert R. Williams, figured out the entire atomic structure to the last atom. Then it was possible to give Vitamin B_1 an official name. The atomic structure included the amine group which Funk had detected twenty years before. It also included a sulfur atom, and, since the Greek word for sulfur is "theion," it was named "thiamine" (THY-ah-meen). Chemists always use "thiamine" now instead of the old-fashioned "Vitamin B_1."

Other members of the B complex received new names as the atom arrangements in their molecules were worked out. Part of the molecule of Vitamin B_2 turned out to have the atom arrangement of the molecule of a sugar known as "ribose." Vitamin B_2 was also yellow in color and the Latin word for yellow is "flavus." Vitamin B_2 was therefore named "riboflavin" (ri-bo-FLAY-vin).

47

Vitamin B_6 was named "pyridoxine" (pih-rih-DOK-sin) because its atomic structure was like that of a well-known compound called "pyridine" by chemists. The Vitamin B_6 molecule had extra oxygen atoms so "ox" for oxygen was added to its name.

Vitamin B_{12} was named "cyanocobalamine" (SI-ah-no-ko-BAWL-ah-meen). This was because it had an amine group in its molecule, an atom of the metal, cobalt, and also an atom-combination called the "cyanide group."

Some members of the B complex never had a letter-number combination. They were given names instead because it had become fashionable to do so. "Biotin" (BI-oh-tin) comes from the Greek word for "life" because it seems to be found in just about every food derived from living things. "Pantothenic acid" (pan-toh-THEN-ik) comes from Greek words meaning "from everywhere" for the same reason. Folic acid (FOH-lik) comes from the Greek word for "leaf" because it is found in the green leaves of vegetables.

Vitamin C, one water-soluble vitamin that is not part of the B complex, also received a name. It is now called "ascorbic acid" (ah-SKAWR-bik) from Greek words meaning "no scurvy."

The fat-soluble vitamins are still commonly known by the old letter-names, however. We still speak of Vitamin A, Vitamin D, Vitamin E, and Vitamin K.

While chemists were working out the structure of the vitamin molecules in the 1930s, they were also working out the structure of the coenzyme molecules.

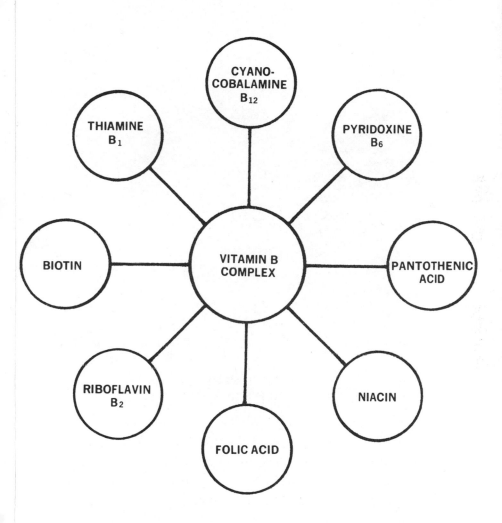

**FOODS CONTAINING
VITAMIN B COMPLEX**

It turned out that parts of the coenzyme molecules consisted of unusual atom-combinations that were not found elsewhere in the body. Furthermore, these unusual atom-combinations were similar to those found in the various vitamins of the B complex. The atom-combination of thiamine was found to exist in one particular coenzyme, and that of riboflavin in another.

Here is what chemists decided must be the answer. Plants could make all the different atom-combinations they needed from the very simple molecules they got from the outside world. They could even make the unusual atom-combinations of the coenzymes.

Most animals, however, could not make the unusual atom-combinations for themselves. They needed so little of them that they could pick them up ready-made in the plant food they ate and store them away in the muscles, the liver, the kidney, and other places.

A vitamin, then, can sometimes be an unusual atom-combination needed to build up a coenzyme. Ordinarily, it comes from food. Only a tiny bit of vitamin is required to make the coenzyme.

If, for any reason, the vitamins were missing from the food, the coenzyme could not be manufactured in the body. That meant certain enzymes could not do their work, and certain chemical reactions could not take place. Consequently, the animal would grow ill and eventually die.

This connection between coenzymes and vitamins enabled chemists to work out the structure of a particular vitamin molecule. In the middle 1930s, various chemists showed that the coenzyme that had first been studied by Harden had an unusual atom-combination called "nicotinic acid" (NIH-koh-TIN-ik) as part of its molecule. It was called that because it had first been obtained by chemists in 1925 by breaking up the molecule of nicotine, a chemical found in tobacco.

Was it possible that this unusual atom-combination was a vitamin? One vitamin that had not yet had its structure figured out was the P-P factor that prevented pellagra in human beings and blacktongue in dogs. The thought occurred to an American chemist, Conrad Arnold Elvehjem (EL-vuh-yem), that nicotinic acid might be the P-P factor. In 1937, Elvehjem gave a dog with blacktongue a single dose of one-thousandth of an ounce of nicotinic acid. The dog was cured.

Doctors were worried that people might think that, since nicotinic acid sounded like "nicotine," there were vitamins in tobacco and that smoking was good for the health. (It isn't!) It would be too bad if they thought so because actually nicotinic acid and nicotine are two entirely different substances, even if the names are similar.

To prevent confusion, doctors combined the first two letters of "nicotinic" and the first two letters of "acid" and added "in." That gave them "niacin" (NI-uh-sin) and this is the name that is almost always used for the P-P factor, instead of nicotinic acid.

Only the vitamins of the B complex are connected with coenzymes, as far as we know. We understand very little about how the other vitamins work.

Vitamin A takes part in the chemical reactions in your eye that make it possible for you to see dim light. That is why, when it is missing, people suffer from "night-blindness."

Vitamin D has something to do with the way the body transfers minerals from the blood to the bones.

Vitamin K has something to do with the way blood forms a clot. We don't know the details, though.

As for Vitamin C and Vitamin E, we have no idea at all what chemical reactions either one works with, or how.

Someday chemists and doctors may find out.

5 Vitamins and Man

THE DISCOVERY OF VITAMINS changed the way in which people ate. People began to realize that it was not enough to eat until you were filled up. Food could satisfy hunger and yet, if it lacked vitamins, you could become unhealthy. People began to make sure they ate at least some of the food that contained each important vitamin.

For instance, Vitamin A is found in leafy vegetables, milk, butter, eggs, and liver. Vitamin D is found in cod-liver oil. The various vitamins of the B complex are found in milk, meat, eggs, liver, grain, and vegetables. Vitamin C is found in tomatoes and in the juice of citrus fruits.

It was also found that food could be treated so as to improve its vitamin content in some ways.

Although few foods contain Vitamin D, many have substances that are *like* Vitamin D. When these foods are exposed to sunlight, the atoms in the Vitamin D-like substances are rearranged and they become actual Vitamin D. Ordinary milk, for instance, has no Vitamin D and cannot prevent rickets. If exposed to

**FOODS CONTAINING
VITAMIN A**

sunlight in the right way, it develops Vitamin D and can then prevent rickets.

In fact, people have substances like Vitamin D in their own bodies. These substances do not keep them from developing rickets. However, if people go out into the sunlight, the substances do turn to Vitamin D. For this reason, children who have no Vitamin D in their diet will *not* develop rickets if they, at least,

**FOODS CONTAINING
VITAMIN C**

receive some sunshine. Vitamin D has come to be known as the "sunshine vitamin."

The new knowledge about vitamins also changed cooking habits. For instance, it was discovered that food soaked in water too long while cooking lost some of the B complex vitamins. If the food was heated too long, some of its Vitamin C was destroyed.

**VITAMIN D
FROM SUNSHINE**

In the 1930s, however, people worried less about the vitamins in food. Once chemists figured out the atomic structure of the vitamin molecules, they found out how to make those molecules in the laboratory.

In 1933, Vitamin C was made in the laboratory by a Swiss chemist named Tadeus Reichstein (RIKE-shtine). In 1936, Vitamin A was made in the laboratory; in 1937, thiamine was made in the laboratory, and so on.

The vitamins made in the laboratory were exactly the same as the vitamins found in food and did their work in exactly the same way. This meant that extra vitamins from the laboratory could be added to the food that people bought. Bread could have extra thiamine and niacin. Milk could have extra Vitamin D. Fruit juices could have extra Vitamin C.

It wasn't even necessary to put the vitamins into the food. The vitamins could be put together in the proper way and sold in drugstores in the form of pills.

It is very common now to buy vitamin pills and to take a certain amount every day. If a person does this, the vitamin content of his food is less important.

Are vitamin pills safe? The water-soluble vitamins can be taken in fairly large quantities without harm. The body gets rid of them if there is more than it needs. In fact, some people think that particularly large quantities of Vitamin C can prevent us from catching colds.

The fat-soluble vitamins are another matter. The body cannot get rid of fat-soluble substances as easily

TADEUS REICHSTEIN

as it can water-soluble substances. If more Vitamin A or Vitamin D is taken in than the body needs, it accumulates in the tissues and can do harm.

On the whole, then, it would not be wise to take more vitamin pills than you need. In fact, a good diet of food containing all the vitamins may be best of all since there is no danger of getting too much of any particular vitamin.

The discovery of vitamins has been of great importance to all of us. The proper use of vitamins is one of the reasons why children today grow taller and stronger than children did fifty or a hundred years ago. It is one of the important reasons why people live longer and are healthier.

VITAMIN PILLS

INDEX